My Persona Book

By Erica McGraw

My Personal Prayer Book

Author: Erica McGraw
Editors: Anjeanette Alexander & Tamara Walters
Publication Services: Kingdom News Publication Services, LLC.

DISCLAIMER
All the material contained in this book is provided for educational and informational purposes only. No responsibility can be taken for any results or outcomes resulting from the use of this material.

While every attempt has been made to provide information that is both accurate and effective, the author does not assume any responsibility for the accuracy or use/misuse of this information.

Printed in the United States of America.
ISBN 978-1955127004

This book belongs to:

_____

From:

_____

Date:

_____

"For God so loved the world that He gave His only begotten Son, that whosoever believes in Him should not perish, but have everlasting life."

John 3:16

INTRODUCTION

This is your personal prayer book so you can pray for your family, friends, and community. Ask an adult to assist you in completing your personal prayers.

Each color represents one day of the week. So, each night before bed, choose the day of the week that it is and pray the prayer. By completing each color daily, you will begin praying on a weekly basis for your loved ones, your friends, and your community.

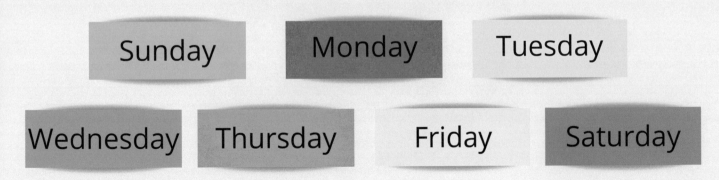

Sunday   Monday   Tuesday

Wednesday   Thursday   Friday   Saturday

SOMETHING TO REMEMBER

Only adults are to write in your book or assist you in writing in your book. You shouldn't write or color in your book without the assistance of an adult. You want to keep your book nice so you can pray all your prayers.

JUST SO YOU KNOW

God already knows everything about you, but this is your personal prayer book and we want to make sure you don't forget anyone. Fill it in with the names of your loved ones, friends, and important people so no one is missed during your times of prayer.

WHAT IS PRAYER

Prayer is simply talking to God. It's telling Him about your day, asking Him to heal you and your loved ones, or seeking help. He is always with you and knows your needs.

DO YOU KNOW WHO JESUS IS?

Jesus is God's own son.

When he was on earth, many miracles he had done.

He healed the sick, provided food, helped the poor,

Taught the people and did so much more.

Many did not listen to him.

That's what God calls sin.

People mistreated the son of God, and it made Jesus sad.

He would forgive them for whatever they did bad.

Jesus came to save the world.

He died on the cross for every boy and girl.

He rose from the grave and is living again.

Jesus is our friend till the very end.

SALVATION PRAYER

Dear God,

I believe that your son, Jesus Christ died on the cross for my sins.
Please forgive me of all my wrong doings.
I believe that you are alive and that you are my savior.
I ask you to be leader of my life now and forever.
Come into my heart, so we will never part.

Amen!

SUNDAY
PRAYING FOR YOUR FAMILY

Everyone has a family. Some families are small, and some are large. Some have both their mommy and daddy, and others may only have a mommy or a daddy. Yet others may be completely different. Some children do not have their mommy and/or daddy that they live with, but they have a guardian who is someone special to love and cares for them.

Today and every Sunday, you are going to pray for your family. It's time to tell us about your family.

Also, some families have pets that are part of their family. Please don't forget to tell us about your pets.

MY FAMILY...

My name is _____.

I have a mommy (guardian); her name is _____.

I have a daddy (guardian); his name is _____.

I have _____ brother(s), _____.

I have _____ sister(s), _____.

I have _____ dog(s), _____.

I have _____ cat(s), _____.

MY FAMILY PRAYER...

Dear God,

Thank you for my family. They make me so happy. I ask that you keep us safe tonight until the morning light. Protect us during the days and help us to keep your ways. God thank you for being our provider, and for food, shelter, peace, joy and laughter. To my family, you are so kind. Help us to love you with all our heart and mind.

Amen!

MONDAY
PRAYING FOR YOUR SCHOOL

School is a fun place to go. You get to meet your teacher and classmates, and all learn new things together. Your teacher becomes a very special person in your life, and you begin to grow from a little child to one who knows so much more.

Classmates become your friends and you always want to watch out and pray for them.

Let us know about your school, teacher, and friends.

MY SCHOOL...

My name is _____.

The name of my school is _____.

My teacher's name is _____.

My friends' names are _____
_____
_____.

My favorite things to learn at school are_____
_____
_____.

MY SCHOOL PRAYER...

Dear God,

You are so amazing. Thank you for my school. I pray that my friends and I will follow all the rules. Continue to protect my school from any danger. Please remember to help my teacher. Let my teachers' dreams come true and help them to trust in you. Please let my teachers be wise in their ways. Give them peace and prosperity throughout their days.

Help my friends to study and do well. Of your goodness, help them to tell. Thank you that they are smart and intelligent. Help them all to be confident. Lord, your beautiful name I adore. I pray my entire school will love you more and more.

Amen!

TUESDAY
PRAYING FOR MY NEIGHBORS

Where you live is very important. A home is a place of safety, love, and neighbors. Sometimes your neighbors become great friends and almost just like your family.

It is important to know those who live around you, so they can watch out and help keep you safe and protected.

Let's learn about your neighbors and neighborhood.

MY NEIGHBORS/NEIGHBORHOOD...

My home is located in (city/state), _____.

I live in (circle one) a house / an apartment / other.

I know some of my neighbors; their name are _____
_____.

Some of the fun activities we do with our neighbors are _____
_____
_____
_____
_____.

MY NEIGOBORHOOD PRAYER...

Dear God,

You are so wonderful. Please cover my neighborhood. Help all my neighbors to do good. Give them the strength to work each day and empower them in every way. Any problem that my neighbors face, you are never late. Help them to trust in you and wait. Jesus, you are our creator and healer. If any of my neighbors are sick, I pray they will become better really quick. Your word tells me to love my neighbor as myself. I pray my neighbors will be kind to me and everyone else. My neighborhood is blessed. Continue to give them peace and rest.

Amen!

WEDNESDAY
PRAYING FOR MYSELF

You are always with you. No way to get from being with you. You have to like yourself and even love yourself. As you are praying for others, it's also good to speak to God and ask Him to cover and protect you.

God is always with you, and He knows everything about you. So go ahead and share those things in your heart with Him. His Word teaches us, He will never leave you. He is with you always.

Let's learn a little more about you!

THIS IS WHO I AM...

Place your picture here.

My name is _____.

I am _____ years old.

I have _____ hair and _____ eyes.

My favorite things to do are_____
_____.

My least favorite things to do are _____
_____.

I have a dream to be _____.

MY PRAYER FOR ME...

Dear God,

You are my King. To you, my praises I bring. Thank you for all that you have done. You see my dreams and visions. With your help, I can accomplish them all. With you by my side, I will never fall. Nothing is too hard for you Jesus. In you, I trust. I am confident that I will succeed. Thank you for being my strength and shield.

Amen!

THURSDAY
PRAYING FOR EXTENDED FAMILY

You probably have some people that you love, but they don't live with you. These people are grandparents, aunts and uncles, cousins, and even some really good friends that you love just like a family member.

Let's learn about your extended family.

MY EXTENDED FAMILY...

My grandma's name is _____.

My grandpa's name is _____.

My aunt and uncle's names are _____
_____.

My cousin's names are _____
_____.

Other family members are _____
_____.

MY PRAYER FOR MY EXTENDED FAMILY...

Dear God,

You are mighty and strong. My family needs you all day long. On your name I call, please protect them all. Help them in all they do and let them to grow more loving too. I pray that your angels will encamp around them. Please guide them out of every problem. Pour out your peace on my family. Give them strength and let them be happy.

Amen!

FRIDAY
PUBLIC FIGURES & MILITARY

We are to pray for those in charge of our government including federal, state and city. Also on a daily basis, there are others who have jobs that protect our rights, our communities, and they are heroes. These people are police officers, firefighters, doctors, nurses, and so many others.

Another group of people you want to pray for is our military personnel as well as our veterans. A veteran is a former member of the armed forces. They served in one of the five branches of the military; the Army, Navy, Air Force, Marine Corps, or Coast Guard. The role of the military is to protect our country, the United States of America.

Do you know anyone who helps to protect you? Please put their names in your personal prayer book, so you can remember to pray for them. - 18 -

PUBLIC FIGURES

U.S. President   U.S. Vice President   Governor

Police Chief   Fire Chief   Military Personnel

Doctors   Nurses   Mayors   Postal Workers

Is there anyone else you can think of to pray for? If so, please write their name or title _____

_____

_____

MY PRAYER FOR
PUBLIC FIGURES AND MILITARY...

Dear God,

You are so kind in every way. Thank you for giving these people the strength to work each day. I ask you, God up above, to protect them with your love. I pray you will help them in their trouble and let their blessings double. Let the leaders who tell the soldiers when to fight, only do so when it is right. Like David and the Israelites who fought for the Lord, let the soldiers fight in one accord.

Amen!

SATURDAY
PRAYING FOR MY CHURCH

God has given us pastors after His own heart to watch over all of us. A pastor is one who called by God to watch over others and teach them the ways of God.

When you are a member of the church, the Pastor watches over the members, which is called a congregation, often referred to as a church family.

It's time to share about your church.

MY CHURCH

The name of my church is _____.

My pastor's name is _____.

My Sunday School Teacher's name is _____.

Do you have a favorite Bible verse? If so, please share it here:

_____

_____

_____

_____

MY PRAYER FOR MY CHURCH...

Dear God,

You are faithful. I pray my church will receive and follow the word. Help us to share your goodness and let it be heard. Destroy the enemy's plans. I place my church in your hands. Cover my pastor and Sunday school teacher with your wings. Bless them with many great things. Jesus, help the entire congregation to draw nearer to you. Please bless them in all they do.

Amen!

DON'T FORGET TO PRAY FOR OUR WORLD!

Made in the USA
Columbia, SC
06 November 2024

45782781R00018